THE **COW**
IN
APPLE TIME

ROBERT FROST

Illustrated by Dean Yeagle

Beekman & Hathaway

Requests for permission to make copies of this work should be mailed to the following address:
Permissions Department, Beekman & Hathaway
P.O. Box 2355, Amherst, Massachusetts 01004-2355

www.beekmanandhathaway.com

Library of Congress Control Number 2004108348
Frost, Robert, 1874-1963.
The cow in apple time/written by Robert Frost; illustrated by Dean Yeagle.
Summary: A cow eats fallen fruit in an apple orchard and runs amok.
ISBN 0-9758970-1-2

2 4 6 8 10 9 7 5 3 1

The illustrations in this book were created with a number two pencil, Photoshop and a Power Mac G4.
The text type was set in Perpetua and Comic Sans MS.
Printed in China
This book was printed on acid-free, 140 gsm, Japanese matte art paper.
Art Direction and Production: Christopher Duran Comer
Layout: Janice M. Phelps

Very special thanks to Matt, Colleen and Jameson Secovich.

Something inspires the only cow of late

To make no more of a wall than an open gate,

And think no more
    of wall-builders than fools.

Her face is flecked
with pomace and
she drools

A cider syrup.

Having tasted fruit,

She scorns a pasture withering to the root.

She runs from tree to tree where lie and sweeten

The windfalls spiked
with stubble
and worm-eaten.

She leaves them bitten when she has to fly.

She bellows on a knoll against the sky.

Her udder shrivels and the milk goes dry.

THE COW IN APPLE TIME

Something inspires the only cow of late
To make no more of a wall than an open gate,
And think no more of wall-builders than fools.
Her face is flecked with pomace and she drools
A cider syrup. Having tasted fruit,
She scorns a pasture withering to the root.
She runs from tree to tree where lie and sweeten
The windfalls spiked with stubble and worm-eaten.
She leaves them bitten when she has to fly.
She bellows on a knoll against the sky.
Her udder shrivels and the milk goes dry.

DIRECT PAYMENTS AND PERSONAL BUDGETS

Putting personalisation into practice

Jon Glasby and Rosemary Littlechild

Revised and substantially updated second edition

This edition published in Great Britain in 2009 by

The Policy Press
University of Bristol
Fourth Floor
Beacon House
Queen's Road
Bristol BS8 1QU
UK

Tel +44 (0)117 331 4054
Fax +44 (0)117 331 4093
e-mail tpp-info@bristol.ac.uk
www.policypress.org.uk

North American office:
The Policy Press
c/o International Specialized Books Services (ISBS)
920 NE 58th Avenue, Suite 300
Portland, OR 97213-3786, USA
Tel +1 503 287 3093
Fax +1 503 280 8832
e-mail info@isbs.com

British Library Cataloguing in Publication Data
A catalogue record for this book is available from the British Library.

Library of Congress Cataloging-in-Publication Data
A catalog record for this book has been requested.

ISBN 978 1 84742 317 7 paperback
ISBN 978 1 84742 318 4 hardcover

Cover design by Qube Design Associates, Bristol
Front cover image © Kevin Chettle. The image used on the front cover is from a painting entitled 'Seeing the seaside which I never saw before', by Kevin Chettle.

The series of Kevin's paintings can be viewed at http://www.bild.org.uk/01kevin_chettle0.htm and portray a moving account of his life from living in a long-stay institution to independence. Kevin now lives in the community and earns his living through giving lectures and selling his paintings.

Printed and bound in Great Britain by Hobbs the Printers, Southampton